How to Raise and Train
BUDGERIGARS

By WILLIAM H. ALLEN, Jr.
Photography LOUISE VAN DER MEID

Distributed in the U.S.A. by T.F.H. Publications, Inc., 211 West Sylvania Avenue, P.O. Box 27, Neptune City, N.J. 07753; in England by T.F.H. (Gt. Britain) Ltd., 13 Nutley Lane, Reigate, Surrey; in Canada to the book store and library trade by Clarke, Irwin & Company, Clarwin House, 791 St. Clair Avenue West, Toronto 10, Ontario; in Canada to the pet trade by Rolf C. Hagen Ltd., 3225 Sartelon Street, Montreal 382, Quebec; in Southeast Asia by Y.W. Ong, 9 Lorong 36 Geylang, Singapore 14; in Australia and the south Pacific by Pet Imports Pty. Ltd., P.O. Box 149, Brookvale 2100, N.S.W., Australia. Published by T.F.H. Publications, Inc. Ltd., The British Crown Colony of Hong Kong.

CONTENTS

©1959, 1978 T.F.H. Publications, Inc.

ISBN 0-87666-415-X

INTRODUCTION

By far the most popular cage bird ever kept by man is the Australian Shell Parakeet or Budgerigar ("Budgie" as it is popularly called). No other bird could more richly deserve this popularity, for the Budgie is an amusing pet, often learning to talk, do tricks and whistle as well as its larger Parrot cousins. It is hardy, prolific, easy to breed, available in a large variety of colors, and is inexpensive to obtain and to care for. What other pet has all of these attributes? Furthermore, the Budgie has few if any of the disadvantages of other pets. They are not overly noisy. They are clean, and do not dig holes in the neighbor's yard. They are all-around pets for the apartment dweller and for the family that lives in the country. For those for whom space is at a premium, the Budgerigar offers the advantage of being easily and profitably raised in a small area. Because of all the colors and color combinations in which Budgies have been bred, this bird is the geneticist's and bird lover's delight.

All of this makes the Budgerigar a tremendously popular little bird. Its popularity is nothing new but has seen a marked increase in the past several years. At present the Budgerigar not only exceeds in popularity all other cage birds, but also rivals the popularity of such unfailingly popular pets as dogs and cats. There are more than 12,000,000 Budgies kept as pets in America.

The Budgerigar is a native of Australia, where it is found in big flocks over a considerable portion of the tropical section of that continent. It lives and breeds in large colonies so that, even in captivity, best results in breeding are obtained if two or more pairs are kept in close proximity to each other. The normal color of the wild birds is light green but there are some yellow specimens. The wide variety of colors apparent today all derive from the original light green.

The wild bird may be described as follows: it is light green with a lemon-yellow face and throat. There are three black spots on each side of the throat. The wing and back markings are black and yellow. Each feather is edged in yellow which gives the over—all appearance of waving or undulating lines. The scientific Latin name, *Melopsittacus undulatus*, is partially derived from this undulating appearance. The individual feathers somewhat resemble small shells; hence the name "Shell Parakeet." The long, pointed tail feathers are blue-green in color.

The name "Budgerigar" is derived from a word in the language of the Australian aborigines. It has been variously written in English as "Betcherrygah," "Boodgereegar," "Betchcerrygar" and other similar spellings. These words have been translated as "good bird," "pretty bird," "good food." It is easy to see how our current spelling, "Budgerigar," was arrived at and how it has been shortened to the popular name

A gray wing blue Budgerigar. Photo by Mervin Roberts

A yellow face rainbow blue opaline Budgerigar. This color
variety is very rare. Photo by Mervin Roberts

"Budgie." The first live specimens were brought from Australia to England in 1840 by the famous naturalist John Gould, and a few were brought to the United States a short time later. Budgerigars are often erroneously referred to as "Love Birds." The true love birds are found in Africa, though, and bear little resemblance to the Budgerigar.

This work has been written for the fancier, breeder and pet owner. Its purpose is to provide a handbook and guide which will answer questions and increase the enjoyment you will get from the fascinating hobby or vocation of Budgie raising. If you want to know how to breed a particular color or how to deal with French Moult, you will find the answers here. If you would like to know how to tame your pet bird, this book will again be of help to you.

HOW TO BREED PARAKEETS

The first step in breeding Parakeets is to be sure to obtain true pairs. This may seem to be an obvious and therefore unnecessary thing to mention. However, all too often an unscrupulous or an uninformed dealer will sell to the unsuspecting novice two birds of the same sex. This is easily avoided for the sexes in Budgerigars are readily distinguished.

HOW TO SEX PARAKEETS

Budgerigars have above the beak a bit of waxy skin containing the nostrils. This bit of skin is called the cere. In the adult male birds the cere is deep sky blue in color. In the females the cere is grayish-white, tan or a deep chocolate brown. Most mature Budgerigar hens in good condition will have a deep, chocolate-brown cere. However some hens, no matter how healthy, never develop the deep brown cere but achieve only a pale tan. This does not mean that they are not in breeding condition; it is merely an individual peculiarity. A white cere with bluish edge usually indicates a hen that is not in breeding condition. It may even indicate poor health.

Unfortunately young birds are not quite so easily sexed. When they emerge from the nest box, both sexes have pale blue ceres. As they reach maturity the blue of the cere of the young males deepens, while that of the females grows paler and then turns almost white before turning brown. Usually this change begins to take place almost immediately, so that even at a very early age it is easy to pick the females by the lighter color of their ceres.

In the sex-linked colors it is easy to tell the sexes of the young birds while they are still in the nest box, as soon as the color is known. This will be explained later when sex linkage is taken up fully.

BREEDING AGE

Another factor to consider before beginning to breed the birds you have obtained is their age. Many young birds develop rapidly and by the time they reach six months of age are apparently mature and ready for breeding. Others mature more slowly and are ten or eleven months old before they appear to be mature. In either case it is unwise to let them breed and raise a family before they are about a year old. To do so will not only endanger their health but might also result in young of inferior quality. There is no particular advantage in waiting longer than a year before breeding them.

As far as maximum breeding age is concerned no hard and fast rule can be laid down. This must depend on the circumstances in each individual case. Some birds make good breeders until they are five or six years old, some until they are considerably older. The care and diet the bird had undoubtedly play some part. Heredity is another important factor. Longevity in birds is as variable as in humans and other animals, though seven years is a good average.

WHEN TO BREED YOUR PARAKEET

The general health and breeding condition of the birds should be taken into consideration before setting them up for breeding. Those selected for breeding at any given time should have had several months' rest since raising their last nest of young. They should not be moulting. Their feathers should be smooth and their eyes should be bright and alert. They should be bursting with energy. The cocks should have deep blue ceres while the hens' ceres should be chocolate-brown and rough in appearance. As has been mentioned previously some hens may never have deep brown ceres. If their ceres are a light tan and they seem to be healthy and in good condition otherwise, it is safe to breed them. If the cere is white it is better to wait as this may be a sign of ill health or immaturity.

Parakeets are not seasonal breeders as are many other birds. They will breed at any time of the year and may be allowed to do so in indoor aviaries or breeding cages, or, outdoors in climates that are warm the year around. Since they are not seasonal breeders chances are that not all of your Parakeets will be through with their moult and in breeding condition at the same time. This being true, you will be able to set some of your birds up for breeding as they come into condition and make no attempt to have all of your pairs raising families at the same time.

In any case it is wise to limit each pair to two nests per year or at most three. If you do not set a limit on their breeding frequency, Budgies will raise nest after nest until they are completely exhausted from their efforts. Offspring of inferior quality result from overbred stock.

Adult birds not set up for breeding need plenty of light and space so they can get adequate exercise and build themselves up again after the de-

An albino
Budgerigar.
Note the red
eyes, the sign of
a true albino.

A blue
Harlequin
Budgerigar.

A yellow-green Budgerigar. Photo by Mervin Roberts

manding job of raising a family. If possible it is wise to have the males and females in two separate flights when they are not set up for breeding. This will also insure that the birds will not choose their mates and breed indiscriminately. If space permits, it is advantageous to maintain the young birds in a flight by themselves. However, the separate flight cages for the adult males, females, and for the young are not absolutely necessary. Many fanciers do not have space for all of this extra housing and prefer to raise a few high quality birds. They seem to get along just about as well and produce birds of equal quality with those who have plenty of flight space.

WHAT BREEDING FACILITIES SHOULD YOU PROVIDE FOR YOUR BIRDS?
CAGE VS. AVIARY BREEDING

The breeding and nesting facilities that you should provide for your birds depends on several factors. First of all, if you are interested in breeding birds of known ancestry, or if you are interested in color breeding where you are trying to get offspring of a particular color or shade, then cage breeding is a must. In cage breeding a pair of birds, carefully chosen for color or other characteristics, is put into a breeding cage and provided with a nest box. In this way when offspring do arrive there is no doubt about their parentage. This can be very important in certain phases of color breeding for two birds may look alike but one may carry recessive characteristics of other non-obvious colors that may be passed on to successive generations. The importance of this will be brought out even more strongly in the section dealing with Color Breeding. Heredity may also be important in the breeding of show stock and cage breeding is necessary here too.

AVIARY OR COLONY BREEDING

Aviary or colony breeding may be used where there is no particular interest in the color or heredity of the young birds. In this type of breeding several pairs of birds are selected and put into a large flight cage or aviary where they are provided with nest boxes and allowed to go to work laying eggs and raising families at random. As male Budgies are notorious for infidelity to their mates there is almost no way of being absolutely certain of the ancestry of the young birds in aviary breeding. There may be some exceptions to this when birds with sex-linked color characteristics are involved. This will be more readily understood when we take up sex linkage a little later. Unless the parentage of the young is important it makes little difference as to whether or not the fatherhood of the young in a given nest is exactly known.

Another factor that may enter into your choice of facilities is available space. If you are limited as to space it is easier to find space for a number of small cages than it is for a large one. This is particularly true during the winter months when you have all of your birds indoors.

No matter which breeding facilities you choose you will want to closely supervise your birds and not allow them to raise too many nests per year or to breed at too young an age. One danger of the aviary method is that often the young birds are left in the aviary with the parents and those that mature early may start raising their own families when they are only 5 or 6 months old. Another danger is that the birds may raise nest after nest unless they are prevented from doing so. The ultimate result of either of these practices will be overworked parents and weak, inferior young that will be worthless as pets or breeders and will be subject to various diseases, some of which may be communicable to man. You never have to worry about this possibility with strong healthy stock that is well cared for.

When the time comes for setting up the chosen pairs for breeding they should be introduced to their breeding quarters. If these quarters are to be cages each pair should be put in its cage alone but within sight of other pairs that are also in breeding cages. It is essential that a pair of birds not be isolated where they cannot see and hear other Parakeets. In their wild state Budgerigars are colony breeders and they will not readily breed if isolated from others of their kind. It is, therefore, essential to have at least two pairs before undertaking to breed Budgies. There may be exceptional birds that will go to nest and raise a family when alone but they are rare indeed . . . most will not.

If the breeding quarters are to be an aviary the chosen pairs should be put into the aviary together. Under no circumstances should an extra unmated hen be put into an aviary with mated pairs. To do so is to invite trouble in the form of fights, ruined eggs, and killed young. Hens are extremely jealous and vindictive and an extra one in a breeding colony is almost sure trouble. On the other hand an extra cock would probably do no harm and might even stimulate the other pairs to go to nest a little sooner.

NEST BOXES

After the birds have been in their breeding quarters for several days to a week it is time to provide them with nest boxes. When breeding a pair in individual cages it is necessary to provide only one nest box for each cage. However, when several pairs are put together into an aviary it is best to put up several more nest boxes than there are pairs in the enclosure. This way the hens have a chance to choose between boxes and the fights that normally ensue when two hens choose the same box, and there is not much more to choose from, may be avoided.

A green opaline
Budgerigar

A clear wing
green opaline
Budgerigar

A mauve opaline Budgerigar

A cobalt fallow Budgerigar. Note clear red eye.

13

For the individual who is only interested in breeding a pair of birds, this type of large cage with attached nest box will serve the purpose well.

After a few days the hen may be seen to disappear into the nest box at frequent intervals and she will spend more and more time in the nest box. Until one or more eggs are layed she will always come out of the box to sleep. During this period of adjustment preparatory to breeding and parenthood the birds are extremely sensitive and should be disturbed as little as possible. Even the cage should be left uncleaned and the birds disturbed only to replenish their food and water supply daily. If disturbed unduly at this point the hen might not lay or might lay her eggs on the cage floor instead of the nest box. The eggs layed might also be broken, or holes pecked in them.

If left undisturbed the hen should lay in due time—probably in about 10 days to two weeks or maybe not quite that long. Budgerigar hens usually lay in the afternoon and the hen begins sitting on the nest day and night after the first egg is laid. She will lay an egg every other day until she has laid 5 or 6 eggs. For the second or third nest during a season considerably more eggs may be laid. The incubation period for Budgerigars is 18 days. As the hen starts setting with the arrival of the first egg and lays on alternate days the eggs will also hatch on alternate days so that some of the young in the nest may be as much as a week older than the others.

THE INCUBATION PERIOD

During the time that the hen is setting on eggs and staying in the nest box, her body undergoes a slight change so that she will not foul her nest. Her excrement is not expelled as often as normally but accumulates in her body and is discharged when she leaves the nest box for a few minutes every 8 hours or more. When the excrement is discharged at these intervals it is entirely different in appearance from that which is normally expelled. It is extremely large and soft.

It is not difficult to ascertain when the first chick hatches for the parents are noticeably excited and the high pitched squeeky voice of the baby may be heard when he is just a few hours old. Hatching usually occurs in the early morning but may take place any time during the day. The other eggs in the nest will hatch on alternate days as their times come.

When first looking at a newly hatched baby Budgie it is almost impossible to believe that it will, in just a few weeks time, develop into something beautiful. A newly hatched Budgie is little and red and ugly. At first glance it appears to be all eyes, which are closed, and beak, which is probably open, calling for food. It has neither down nor feathers when it hatches but soon grows a thick crop of grey or white down which, as times goes on, gives way to the developing feathers. At five weeks of age the baby birds are fully developed.

HOW YOUNG BUDGIES ARE FED

The hen Budgerigar feeds her young in much the same manner as pigeons feed their young. They are fed on a substance regurgitated from the hen's crop. This substance is called *Budgie milk*. They are fed on *Budgie milk* entirely for the first few days of their lives but as time goes on, they begin to receive a few seeds. As they grow older the proportion of seeds increases until eventually they are fed nothing but seeds. The really remarkable thing is that when there are several babies of varying ages in the nest the hen always feeds the youngest first so that he gets the largest proportion of Budgie milk from the top of her crop. The next youngster is fed in turn and gets a few seeds along with his Budgie milk. Then the next and the next according to its needs and stage of development. Each baby in the nest gets different proportions of Budgie milk and solid food.

When they first hatch the baby Budgies are fed about once every 15 minutes day and night but as time goes on the intervals between feed-

A clutch of newborn Budgies. Photo by Mervin Roberts

A normal yellow female Budgerigar. Note the brown cere.
Photo by Mervin Roberts.

A yellow face blue rainbow harlequin. Photo by Mervin Roberts

ings increase. The newly hatched babies are fed while lying on their backs but it is not long until they are able to sit up and stretch out their necks to their mother to be fed. During this period the hen is fed by the cock in the same manner that she uses to feed her babies. She does not leave the nest box to secure food for herself.

THE YOUNG BUDGIE

The fully feathered young Budgie bears little resemblance to the tiny chick that hatched just 5 weeks earlier. It emerges from the nest box as a beautiful bird. Its color closely resembles that of the adult birds except that it is often of a little softer shade. In the normal colored varieties the yellow or white forehead does not occur in the baby birds but instead the black striped feathers on the back and head are also found on their forehead. The beaks of young birds are often streaked with brown or black but this soon disappears, leaving a normal solid colored bill.

When the baby birds are fully feathered their mother stops feeding them so that they are forced to come first to the entrance of the nest box and then to the outside to be fed by their father.

After the young emerge from the nest box it is a good idea to put some bird seed in a shallow dish on the floor of the cage as the babies may have a hard time finding the seed hoppers in the side of the cage for a few days. The young birds that are raised in a cage will probably return to the nest box to sleep for two or three nights. Those raised in a large aviary usually do not leave the nest box until they are able to fly and then they seldom return. As soon as the young birds are eating by themselves it is time to take them away from their parents and put them in a separate cage or aviary.

Chances are that by the time the last baby is ready to leave the nest the hen has already started laying a second clutch of eggs. She will put up with no interference from her young under these circumstances and if they continue to bother her by returning to the nest box she may maim or even kill them.

THE SECOND NEST

Most Budgerigar hens lay a larger second clutch of eggs than the first clutch. When the young from this second nest are ready to leave the nest the hen may begin to lay a third clutch. Chances are that by this time both parents are pretty well run down and exhausted so that these eggs should either be destroyed or moved to the nest of another hen who has only a few eggs. Certainly no more than three nests should be allowed before retiring the parent stock for a well-earned rest.

If anything should happen to one of the parents while there are young in the nest, the other parent, male or female, is perfectly capable of feeding and caring for the young until such time as they are ready to leave the nest. This being true, many fanciers remove the hen after the young of the second clutch are two or three weeks old so that she will not start laying a third clutch. The cock is left to care for the young and he usually does a good job.

On occasion something may happen to both parents or it may be desirable for one reason or another to remove the young birds from one nest and put them in another nest for other birds to care for. These foster parents will usually accept transferred young and feed them providing they have young of their own in approximately the same stage of development. It may be disastrous, however, to put baby birds into a nest where no eggs have hatched as yet. The result would be that the chicks would be unceremoniously murdered.

Where young birds are put with foster parents it is a good idea to watch closely for the first day to make sure that the young birds are being fed. If they are not they will have to be returned to their parents, removed to another nest or hand fed.

BANDING

Many fanciers who raise pedigreed stock will want to put aluminum bands on their birds' legs for the purpose of identification and record-keeping. In fact, banding is now required by the laws of some states for those who are raising Budgies for market.

The time to band the baby birds is when they are about a week old. If the bands are put on before this they will come off in the nest box. If you wait much longer you will not be able to slip the bands on over the feet.

The band may be put on either leg. To put the band on push two of the toes forward and insert the band on them. Push the other two toes backwards and slip the band up the leg. The two toes that are pushed backward may then be pulled out from under the band. A match stick or a toothpick may be of some aid in pulling the toes from under the band.

The aluminum bands with code numbers are available through the various Budgerigar societies and from many local pet dealers. They are an indispensible aid in keeping records for the breeder who is interested in color breeding and in raising show stock.

You must use great care when affixing a band on the leg of a week-old Budgie. Photo by Mervin Roberts

A yellow face clear wing cobalt blue Budgerigar.

A yellow Danish pied (also called harlequin).
Photo by Mervin Roberts.

GENETICS AND COLOR BREEDING

As this does not purport to be a scientific treatise but a guide book for the Parakeet owner and breeder there is no place here for any extended discussion of the laws of genetics or inheritance. Nor is there any place here for scientific discussion of chromosomes or genes. Suffice it to say that it is the genes, carried by the chromosomes, in the cell structure of all birds and animals, including Budgerigars, that determine the inheritance and the inheritable characteristics that are passed on to the offspring. Hence the color, as well as other characteristics, of a given Budgerigar is determined by the chromosomes and genes of the parent birds. The details of how this works, in theory and in practice, can be found by those who are interested in going into it further in scientific works of various kinds.

Budgerigars, like other birds and animals, breed according to the Mendelian laws of inheritance. That is, certain colors are dominant and others are recessive. The dominant characteristics can mask or hide recessive characteristics so that a particular bird may appear to be one color but may have hidden in its makeup the color characteristics that will produce offspring of another color. Such a bird is said to be "split" to the other color. Thus, you may have a green bird that is split to blue. That is the bird is green in appearance but it carries hidden inheritable blue characteristics so that if bred to a blue bird some of the offspring will be blue.

DOMINANT AND RECESSIVE CHARACTERISTICS

It is only the dominant characteristics that can be split. Green is always dominant to everything. Blue is recessive to green but is dominant to white. To put this in a more concrete form you may have a green bird that is split to either blue or white. A white bird, with normal inheritance, cannot be split. In normal non-sex-linked birds these principles apply to both male and female birds.

Using the principles above, which are oversimplified here, you can, if you know something of the ancestry of your breeding stock, predict with reasonable certainty what color offspring you will get from a particular mating. This does not mean to say that you can say accurately what will come from every pair everytime, but you can say that mating birds of a particular color with particular inheritance color characteristics, you can expect over a period of time to have certain results as far as the colors of the young birds raised are concerned. (When considering the various colors individually the best mating for producing birds of certain colors will be given in a later section.) This does not mean that every bird in the nest will be that color or that when it is said that from mating a light green cock to a cobalt hen you should get 50% light green/blue (light green split to blue) young, you can expect every nest of six young birds to have three light green/blue birds. However, over a period of time with a number of such matings you can expect to get 50% light green/blue young.

Occasionally there will appear in a nest of young a bird of an entirely different color from any expected or from anything in the inheritance of either of the parents. This bird in turn will pass on its new color to some of its offspring. Such a bird is called a *mutation*. The wide variety of colors that we have in Budgerigars today are the results of mutations that have occurred from time to time. All of the wild Budgies in their native Australia are a light green. Even in the wild, however, an occasional yellow mutation is seen.

SEX-LINKAGE

As has been pointed out, most colors and characteristics are inherited by both the males and females. Some color characteristics, however, are passed on by the genes contained in the sex chromosomes and these characteristics are linked to the sex of the bird. Hence these characteristics are said to be *sex-linked*. Sex-linked birds when bred to normal colored birds will produce young hens of one color and young cocks of another. Or the young cocks may be split to the sex-linked characteristic but be normal in appearance. The young hens, however, cannot be split to a sex-linked characteristic. If they are normal in appearance they are normal. They may be of the sex-linked color, however. In any case the young hens are just what they appear to be.

The Lutinos, Albinos, Opalines, and Cinnamons are among the sex-linked varieties. Since Lutinos are very common today, they will be used as an example in a table of theoretical expectations, for mating the sex-linked varieties. What is said concerning Lutinos here applies equally to the other sex-linked varieties.

The expectations from mating Lutino and normal birds can be summarized as follows:
1. Lutino cock X Lutino hen = both cocks and hens Lutino
2. Lutino cock X normal hen = Lutino hens and normal/Lutino cocks.
3. Normal/Lutino cock X Lutino hen=Lutino cocks and hens, normal/Lutino cocks, normal hens.
4. Normal/Lutino cock X normal hen=normal/Lutino cocks and normal hens.
5. Normal cock X Lutino hen=normal/Lutino cocks and normal hens.

As has been pointed out earlier this table is not infallible. It will be true in a majority of cases. There may be an occasional variance when the picture is complicated by matings of unusual genetical backgrounds.

It should also be mentioned that there are also non-sex-linked vari-

A normal green male. Note the blue cere.

A normal blue male Budgerigar. Photo by Mervin Roberts.

An olive cinnamon Budgie.

eties of both the Albino and Lutino colors. The sex-linked varieties are, nevertheless, much more common.

Before leaving the subject of genetics it should also be pointed out that other characteristics besides color are inherited. Therefore it is important to get good stock and to take good care of it. Inferior stock will produce inferior young. Good stock will produce good young. It costs no more to feed and care for good stock than it does bad.

COLOR STANDARD OF THE AMERICAN BUDGERIGAR SOCIETY

LIGHT GREEN—Mask: Buttercup yellow of an even tone ornamented on each side of throat with three clearly defined black spots, one of which appears at the base of the cheek patch. Cheek patches: violet. General body color: back, rump, breast, flanks, and under parts bright grass-green of a solid and even shade throughout; markings on cheeks, back of head, neck, and wings black and well defined on a buttercup ground. Tail: long feathers blue-black.

DARK GREEN—As above, but of a dark laurel green body color. Tail: Long feathers darker in proportion.

OLIVE GREEN—As above, but of a dark olive green body color. Tail: long feathers darker in proportion.

LIGHT YELLOW (including Cinnamon Light Yellow) — Mask: Buttercup yellow; back, rump, breast, flanks, wings, and under parts buttercup and as free from green suffusion as possible; primaries lighter than body. Tail: Long feathers lighter than body color.

DARK YELLOW (including Cinnamon Dark Yellow)—As above, but of deeper body color.

OLIVE YELLOW (including Cinnamon Olive Yellow) — As above, but of mustard body color.

SKY BLUE—Mask: Clear white ornamented on each side of throat with three clearly defined black spots, one of which appears at the base of the cheek patch. Cheek patches: violet. General body color: back, rump, breast, flanks, and under parts pure sky blue; markings on cheeks, back of head, neck and wing black and well defined on a white ground. Tail: long feathers blue-black.

COBALT BLUE — As above, but of a rich cobalt-blue body color. Tail: long feathers darker in proportion.

MAUVE — As above, but body color purplish-mauve with a tendency to a pinkish tone. Tail: long feathers darker in proportion.

VIOLET — As sky blue, but of a deep intense violet body color. Tail: long feathers darker in proportion.

WHITES (including Cinnamon Whites) of light suffusion—Mask: White. General body color: back, rump, breast, flanks, and under parts white. Wings and tail pure white.

WHITEWINGS, WHITES OF DEEP SUFFUSION, AND CINNAMON WHITES of deep suffusion (including sky blue, cobalt blue, mauve, violet, and gray) — Mask: White, ornamented on each side of the throat with three gray spots (the paler the better), one of which appears at the base of the cheek patch. General body color: back, rump, breast, flanks, and under parts very heavily suffused body color approximating the normal variety. Wings and tail: pure white. Cheek patches: in every case a pale color of the variety they represent.

GRAYWING LIGHT GREEN — Mask: Yellow, ornamented on each side of throat with three gray spots (the paler the better), one of which appears at the base of the cheek patch. Cheek patches: pale violet. General body color: back, rump, breast, flanks, and under parts pale grass-green. Markings on cheeks, back of neck, and wings should be smoky gray with pale bluish tinge.

GRAYWING DARK GREEN — As above, but of light laurel green body color. Tail: long feathers darker in proportion.

GRAYWING OLIVE GREEN — As above, but of a light olive green body color. Tail: darker still in proportion.

GRAYWING SKY BLUE — Mask: White, ornamented on each side of throat with three clearly defined gray spots, one of which appears at the base of the cheek patch. Cheek patches: light violet. General body color: back, rump, breast, flanks, and under parts clear sky blue. Markings: on cheeks, back of head and wings pure gray, halfway between black and zero. Tail: long feathers grayish blue.

GRAYWING COBALT BLUE — As above, but of a pale blue body color, with tail of corresponding color.

GRAYWING VIOLET — As Graywing Sky Blue, but of a pale violet body color, with tail of corresponding color.

GRAYWING MAUVE — As above, but of a pale mauve body color.

GRAYWING GRAY GREEN — As Graywing Light Green, but with color of light mustard green. Cheek patches: light gray. Tail: long tail feathers deep gray.

GRAYWING GRAY — As Graywing Sky Blue but with body color of pale gray. Tail: feathers deep gray.

CINNAMON LIGHT GREEN — Mask: Yellow, ornamented on each side of throat with three clearly defined cinnamon brown spots, one of which appears at the base of the cheek patch. Cheek patches: violet. General body color: back, rump, breast, flanks, and under parts pale grass green. Markings on cheeks, back of head, neck and wings cinnamon brown well defined on a yellow ground. Tail: long feathers dark blue with brown quill.

A clear body green opaline Parakeet.

A normal blue gray Parakeet.

A yellow face
cobalt blue
Parakeet.

A blue
self-colored
Parakeet.

CINNAMON OLIVE GREEN — As above, but of a light laurel green color. Tail: long feathers darker in proportion.

CINNAMON SKY BLUE — Mask: White, ornamented on each side of the throat with three clearly defined cinnamon brown spots, one of which appears at the base of the cheek patch. Cheek patches: violet. General body color: back, rump, breast, flanks, and under parts pale sky blue. Markings on cheeks, back of head, neck, wings cinnamon brown on white ground. Tail: long feathers blue with brown quill.

CINNAMON COBALT BLUE — As above, but general body color of pale cobalt. Tail: long feathers as above, but cobalt.

CINNAMON MAUVE — As above, but with general body color of pale mauve. Tail: long feathers as above, but mauve.

CINAMON GRAY — As Cinnamon Sky blue, but with body color of pale gray. Tail: long feathers of deep cinnamon shade.

CINNAMON GRAY GREEN — As Cinnamon Light Green, but with body color of pale gray. Tail: long feathers of deep cinnamon shade.

CINNAMON VIOLET — As Cinnamon Sky blue, but general body color of pale violet. Tail: long feathers of pale cinnamon shade. NOTE: In all forms of Cinnamons the male bird carries a deeper shade than the female.

FALLOW LIGHT GREEN — Mask: Yellow, ornamented on each side of throat with three clearly defined brown spots, one of which appears at the base of the cheek patch. Cheek patches: violet. General body color: back, rump, breast, flanks, and under parts yellowish green. Markings on cheeks, back of head, neck and wings dark brown on a yellow ground. Eyes: clear red or plum colored. Tail: long feathers bluish gray.

FALLOW DARK GREEN — As above, but pale laurel green body color. Tail: long feathers darker in proportion.

FALLOW OLIVE GREEN — As above, but with light mustard olive body color. Tail: long feathers darker in proportion.

FALLOW SKY BLUE — Mask: White, ornamented on each side of throat with three clearly defined brown spots, one of which appears at the base of the cheek patch. Cheek patches: violet. General body color: back, rump, breast, flanks, and under parts pale sky blue. Markings on cheeks, back of head, neck, and wings dark brown on a white ground. Eyes: clear red or plum colored. Tail: long feathers bluish gray.

FALLOW COBALT BLUE — As above, but with a warm cobalt blue body color. Tail: long feathers darker in proportion.

FALLOW MAUVE — As above, but with a pale mauve body color of pinkish tone. Tail feathers: darker in proportion.

FALLOW VIOLET — As Fallow Sky Blue, with a pale violet body. Tail: long feathers darker in proportion.

LIGHT FORMS — The committee recognizes the existence of light form of Cinnamon and Fallow, identical to the normal already described, but lighter in body color and markings.

PURE YELLOW RED-EYES (Lutinos)—Buttercup yellow throughout. Eyes: clear red. Tail: long feathers and primaries grayish white.

PURE WHITE RED-EYES (Albinos) — White throughout. Eyes clear red.

YELLOW-WING LIGHT GREEN — Mask: Buttercup yellow, ornamented on each side of throat with three smoky gray spots (the paler the better), one of which appears at the base of the cheek patch. General body color: back, rump, breast, flanks, and, under parts bright grass green. Wings: buttercup yellow. Tail: long feathers pale grass green.

YELLOW-WING DARK GREEN — As above, but with general body color of laurel green. Tail: long feathers darker in proportion.

YELLOW-WING OLIVE GREEN — As above, but with general body color of olive green. Tail: long feathers darker in proportion.

OPALINE LIGHT GREEN — Mask: Buttercup yellow, extending over back of head and merging into general body color at a point level with the butt of wings, where undulations should cease, thus leaving a clear "V" effect between top of wings so desirable in this variety; mask to be ornamented by six large black throat spots, the outer two being partially covered at the base of violet cheek patches. General body color: Mantle (including "V" area or saddle), back, rump, breast, flanks, and under parts bright grass green. Wings: to be iridescent and of the same color as body; markings should be normal and symmetrical, long tail feathers not to be lighter than mantle.

OPALINE DARK GREEN — As above, but of a dark laurel green body color. Tail: long feathers darker in proportion.

OPALINE SKY BLUE — As above, but with a sky blue body color and suffusion, and white mask instead of buttercup yellow. Tail: long feathers not to be lighter than mantle.

OPALINE COBALT BLUE — As Opaline Sky Blue, but of a cobalt blue body color. Tail: long feathers darker in proportion.

OPALINE MAUVE — As Opaline Sky Blue, but of a mauve body color. Tail: long feathers darker in proportion.

OPALINE VIOLET — As Opaline Sky Blue, but of a deep intense violet body color. Tail: long feathers not to be darker than mantle.

OPALINE GRAY — As Opaline Sky Blue, but with body color of solid gray. Tail: long tail feathers not to be lighter than mantle. Cheek patches gray.

OPALINE GRAY GREEN — As Opaline Light Green, but with body

A yellow face
white cobalt
opaline.

A cinnamon
wing green
Parakeet.

color of dull mist green. Tail: long tail feathers not to be lighter than mantle, cheek patches gray.

YELLOW FACE — Mask only: Yellow, otherwise exactly as corresponding white and blue varieties. Note: Yellow-marked feathers in tail permissible.

GRAY — Mask: White, ornamented on each side of throat with three clearly defined black spots, one of which appears at the base of the cheek patch. Cheek patches: gray. General body color: back, rump, breast, flanks, and under parts solid gray. Markings on cheeks, back of head, neck and wings: black and well defined on a white ground. Tail: long feathers blue-black. NOTES The terms Light, Medium, and Dark the sky blue, cobalt blue and mauve forms respectively.

LIGHT GRAY GREEN — This variety conforms to the standard of light green except in the following details: cheek patches gray. General body color: dull mustard green. Tail: long feathers black.

MEDIUM GRAY GREEN — This term denotes the dark green form of the gray.

DARK GRAY GREEN — This form represents the Gray Olive Green. NOTE: The committee does not feel justified at this juncture in describing Medium Gray Green, and Dark Gray Green. As soon as enough data are available, detailed descriptions will be published.

SLATE — Mask: White, ornamented on each side of throat with three clearly defined black spots, one of which appears at the base of the cheek patch. Cheek patches: violet. General body color: back, rump, flanks, and under parts even greenish slate. Markings on cheeks, back of head, neck and wings: black and well defined on a white ground. Tail: long feathers blue-black. NOTE: The terms Light, Medium, and Dark describe the sky blue, cobalt and mauve forms respectively.

LIGHT SLATE GREEN — In every respect as the standard for Light Green, except that the general body color is sage green. NOTE: The terms Light, Medium, and Dark describe the green, dark green, and olive forms respectively.

This concludes the official standard. Here are some of the colors that the fancier has to choose from and ways that he can produce them:

LIGHT GREEN

Any discussion of the colors that have been produced in the Budgerigar must necessarily begin with the light green for it is from this color that all of the other colors have been derived.

As the green is dominant there are not only purebred light green birds but the greens may be split to most any variety, normal or rare. The cocks may be split to any of the sex-linked varieties. The best way to produce good light greens, for the beginner at any rate, is to mate

light green to light green. Later an occasional or an original cross t
another color may be advisable, but for the first few generations ther
will be no necessity of this.

It would be difficult to say that any of the many colors that have bee
developed from the light green, either directly or indirectly, is an in
provement on it. This, of course, would be a matter of opinion but in an
case the light green is a truly beautiful bird.

THE DARK GREEN

Although the green is a beautiful bird in its own right and a
such is quite popular with breeders and pet enthusiasts, perhaps its chie
value is as an aid in breeding cobalt blues of magnificent depth and tone
Dark greens are also valuable for producing good olive greens. Whil
good dark greens can be produced by mating dark green to dark green
a better mating is light green to olive green. Dark green/blue may b
produced by mating light green to cobalt, light green to mauve, ligh
green/blue to cobalt, or olive green to sky blue.

THE OLIVE GREEN

The olive green is the darkest of the green series of Budgerigars. A
good olive is so dark that it is somewhat drab in appearance and cor
sequently olives are not very popular as pets. They are, however, invaluabl
to the color breeder who wants to produce good deep-colored cobalts an
mauves. The best pure olives can be produced by mating olive to olive
Good olive/blue can be produced by mating olive to mauve. The oliv
Budgerigars have been responsible for several mutations.

THE VARIOUS SHADES OF YELLOW

The yellow, like the green in Budgerigars, comes in light, dark an
olives colors. These are all yellow birds but all have a different gree
suffusion.

The ideal in the light yellow is to produce a color as free of th
green suffusion as possible. These pure yellow birds are often referre
to as *buttercup yellow*. The common light yellow with green suffusion i
often seen in the pet shops and is usually referred to as a *Chartreus*
parakeet. It is quite a pretty bird and makes an attractive pet but doe
not measure up to the show standard. The light *buttercup yellow* shoul
not be confused with the Lutino which is a yellow bird with red eyes an
is entirely free of any marking or suffusion whatsoever. The Lutino is
sex-linked variety while the buttercup yellow is not.

The only reliable mating for the production of buttercup yellows i
to mate buttercup to buttercup. If any other color is introduced int
the buttercup strain it is likely to reintroduce the undesirable gree
suffusion.

The dark yellow is yellow with a dark green suffusion and often ha a muddy appearance. A clear specimen is attractive. The best mating is dark yellow to dark yellow.

The olive yellow, as the name implies, is yellow with an olive suffusion. The best mating is olive yellow to olive yellow.

SKY BLUE

The sky blue, the lightest of the blue series of Budgerigars, first made its appearance in a European aviary around 1880. Shortly after that it disappeared and no more were seen until 1910. Today it is one of the prettiest and most popular colors both on the show bench and as a pet. The best mating for the sky blue is to mate sky blue to sky blue. In order to maintain depth of color, stamina and size in a sky blue strain an occasional mating of green/blue to sky blue is advisable.

COBALT

The deep cobalt blue is one of the prettiest colors that we have in the Budgerigar. It first made its appearance in 1921 along with the mauve. The cobalt is a hybrid and consequently never breeds true. A mating of cobalt to cobalt will produce 25% sky blue, 50% cobalt, and 25% mauve. Actually the cobalt is a cross between sky blue and mauve. A good mating is that of sky blue to cobalt which can be expected to produce both sky blue and cobalt progeny in equal numbers. As is the case with the sky blues an occasional cross with a green/blue is advantageous in the production of deep toned cobalts for the show bench.

MAUVE

The mauve is a dark grayish blue in tone and, like the olive, is often somewhat drab when compared with the more brilliant colors. It is consequently not very popular as a pet but is invaluable to the color breeder who wants to deepen the colors of his other birds. The best mating is mauve to mauve with an occasional outcross to a green/blue bird. Some fanciers say that the best mating for the production of good mauves is olive green/blue to mauve. The olive green/blue should have a mauve parent and not a cobalt one.

THE WHITES OF BLUE SUFFUSION

These birds are not actually white but are suffused with a light blue (sky blue, cobalt or mauve) wash. The ideal is to have the lightest possible suffusion so that the birds appear to be almost completely white. In mating them look out for the color of the blue suffusion for they can be expected to produce young with blue suffusion just like their counterparts in the deeper blue series. In breeding whites get the lightest possible birds in order to produce lightly suffused young. The whites of mauve suffusion, particularly in the young birds before the first moult, are often almost as white as an Albino. Usually the suffusion deepens somewhat after the growth of the adult plumage.

VIOLET

The violet is a color of comparitively recent appearance and its genetics have been the subject of a number of controversial articles that make its production sound quite complicated. Actually some rather knotty genetical problems are presented by the violet but the practical breeder can produce some pretty violet birds without bothering himself with trying to understand what the scientific controversy is all about.

As far as the practical breeder is concerned, the violet is a variant of the cobalt and should be treated as such. The rules for cobalt breeding can be followed when dealing with violets. The violet factor is dominant so that it is unnecessary for both parents to carry the violet characteristic in order to produce violet young.

THE YELLOW-FACE BLUE

In view of the fact that the normal blue Budgerigars all have white faces it is somewhat startling to see bright blue, deep sky blue, cobalt or mauve with a striking lemon-yellow face and touches of yellow on the tail and sometimes in the wings. This mutation is a fairly recent one.

The yellow face appears not only on the normal blue Budgerigars but also on those birds that are white with blue suffusions. One of the most breathtakingly beautiful Budgerigars is a yellow-faced white with cobalt suffusion.

The yellow-faced factor is said to be dominant but in actual practice does not always turn out to be so. To be sure, large numbers of yellow-faced young come from nests with only one yellow-faced parent but the surest way to produce yellow-faced blues is to mate yellow-faced blue to yellow-faced blue.

THE GRAYWINGS

The graywings occur in all shades of the green and of the blue series and in violet. The markings, instead of being black as in the normal, should be a smokey gray. In reality the gray of the graywings varies considerably from almost black to an extremely light gray that is almost imperceptable. The ideal is a medium shade of gray. In achieving this shade it is necessary to mate the dark to the light, but even then, the young will sometimes be like one or another of the parents instead of being an intermediate shade. Even two graywings of the right shade may produce some young that are not what they should be as far as the shade of gray is concerned. The graywing factor is recessive to normal so that both parents must carry the graywing factor in order to produce graywing young. One of them may of course be a normal split graywing.

THE CINNAMONS

The cinnamons have been produced in all colors. Their markings are a light cinnamon brown instead of the normal color. When they hatch, young cinnamons have reddish colored eyes but by the time they are two weeks old their eyes are the normal black color.

As has been pointed out earlier the cinnamons are a sex-linked variety and should be bred according to the rules governing sex linkage given in the first part of this chapter.

THE FALLOW

The fallows, a red-eyed variety with light brown markings somewhat resembling the cinnamon, have been bred in all colors. The colors are of a somewhat lighter shade than normal colors. Both pure fallow yellow and pure fallow white with no markings whatsoever have been bred. These resemble the Lutino and Albino so that it is necessary to know the genetical background of the birds in order to know what they are. The fallow is a non-sex-linked variety.

THE ALBINO

The Albino is a clear white bird with red eyes and no markings. There are both sex-linked and non-sex-linked varieties but the most common and popular are the sex-linked birds. Actually the Albino masks some other color in the blue series so that it is necessary to know the inheritance of an Albino for breeding purposes. Many Albinos are inferior to other birds in size, type, and feather structure.

THE LUTINO

If the author had to pick a favorite from among the wide variety of colors that the Budgerigar has been produced in, he believes the Lutino would be it. This striking bird is a clear deep yellow without any markings. The long wing and tail feathers are snowy white. Many Lutinos are superior in size and type and have good feather structure.

As is the case with the Albino, the Lutino has been bred in both sex-linked and non-sex-linked strains. The Lutino masks some color in the green or yellow series so that its ancestry should be known for breeding purposes. Lutinos should not be mated to Lutinos as type and size may suffer in this mating but a split Lutino cock should be mated to a Lutino hen. A dark green makes a good mate for a Lutino as this helps to preserve the deep yellow color.

THE OPALINE

The Opaline is a sex-linked bird that has been bred in all colors. In the Opaline the "V" shaped space on the back between the wings is the same color as the rest of the body and is free of markings. The wings are normally marked.

PIEDS OR HARLEQUINS

Budgerigars that show markings of their recessive color are called *pieds*. Yellow or white birds that have black or colored markings are called *harlequins*. The pieds and harlequins breed according to the

Mendelian laws of inheritance so that a normal bird may be split pied. Several strains of the pieds have been developed and they may vary some in their inheritance. These birds have been quite popular during the past few years.

OTHERS

This is by no means an exhaustive list of the colors and varieties of the Budgerigar. There are a number of others and there are completely new ones that are still appearing from time to time. That is one thing that makes breeding Budgerigars so fascinating.

Among the colors most mentioned above that are now in existence are the English and Australian Grays; the clear wings with no markings on the wings; the white wings or yellow wings with faint markings on the wings; the white flighted or yellow flighted that have normal wing markings except for having white or yellow flight feathers; the brown wings with lighter markings than the cinnamons and with a non-sex-linked inheritance. There are a number of others. No list is ever complete but the most common and the most popular have been taken up here. Even if there were no more than these there are enough to hold the interest and fascination of anyone. By the time you have bred and experimented with all of these colors there will be others. As far as Budgerigars are concerned there will always be new worlds to conquer.

HOW AND WHERE TO HOUSE YOUR BUDGIE

The housing accomodations that you provide for your birds will depend largely upon the space that you have available. The space you provide should have several essential attributes. First of all it should be reasonably dry and not subject to dampness during certain times of the year. It should be free from drafts, or at least the birds should be able to get out of a draft. It will not hurt if there is a breeze through the birds quarters so long as they can out of it whenever they desire, especially when they are roosting at night. The birds should also be able to get out of the direct rays of the sun and out of the rain. The place should not be subject to either extremely hot or extremely cold temperatures. Almost any place that can provide these essentials will be satisfactory. If you have an extra room in your house, an unused attic or basement, an unused garage that meets these standards, any of these can be utilized to house your birds.

Of course if you have available space and capital you can erect a structure especially for your birds. Such a structure would consist of a well-insulated building with flight cages or pens projecting from it. These are ideal but not necessary. Special outdoor aviaries are beyond the means, for one reason or another, of most fanciers and they seem to

Budgie cages should be situated away from the reach of cats, rats and snakes. Put their cage on a birdstand.

get along just about as well and raise equally as good birds as those who have them. A good combination is to have indoor winter quarters, such as an extra room, attic or basement, and an outdoor flight where the birds can be turned out in nice weather. Such an outdoor flight should have a shelter at one end where the birds can get out of the direct rays of the sun and out of a hard rain. (Budgies enjoy a small shower in warm weather.) In climates that are warm the year around such an outdoor flight will be adequate all of the time.

There is one other essential for raising good quality Budgies. *They must be reasonably free from disturbance, particularly at night.* Although Budgies will breed and raise their families in the kitchen closet, or in one corner of the living room, it is difficult to raise first class young under such conditions.

One more thing should be pointed out at this time. Although Budgerigars will breed and raise their families and get along fine in small cages with limited opportunity for exercise, they need exercise when not breeding and should be provided with as much flight space as possible.

The ideal setup is to have three flight cages: one for the adult males, one for the adult females, and one for the young of both sexes after they are able to take care of themselves and before they reach breeding age. The adult males and females are likely to choose their own mates and pair off, and will not readily accept the mates you choose for them at breeding time if they are left in the flights together. This may give you a late start in the breeding season. Then too the young birds get along better if they are kept to themselves until they reach maturity. However, the most important thing is that flight space be provided and that the birds get adequate exercise so if you can only provide one flight cage by all means do so. Provide whatever accomodations you can.

The size of the flight cages will depend on the space available. They should be as large as you can comfortably provide so the space you have will in some measure dictate the size of the flights or aviaries. An aviary seven feet tall is ideal so that you can walk in it, to replenish food or water supply or to catch the birds. If this is not possible, flight cages may be used. Within certain limits, the larger the flight cage, the better it is for your birds. The birds should not be too crowded. It is next to impossible to tell how much space per bird you should allow but one good test is to drive all the birds to the perches at one end of a flight cage. If there is an average space of two inches between the birds then you have not overcrowded them. The flights should have perches at each end but not in the middle so that the birds will have to fly from one end of the cage to the other and thus get maximum wing exercise.

The perches can be of two types. The usual dowels can be used as perches, or the branches from non-poisonous trees such as willow, ash, or fruit trees may be used. If the dowels are used they should be of varying sizes, but not too thick so that the Budgerigars' feet will get a rest and change. Whichever kind of perches you use, they should not be placed so that the birds sitting on one perch can foul another with their excrement.

Either the aviary or the flight cage should be covered by $\frac{1}{4}$- or $\frac{1}{2}$-inch mesh hardware cloth. The frame should be of wood or of the low-cost aluminum that is now on the market.

HOW TO RAISE PARAKEETS COMMERCIALLY

If your goal is to produce the largest possible number of youngs Budgies in the shortest period of time, and if you do not care too much about the inheritance of your birds or that they are of superior quality, then aviary breeding is what you want to do. Aviary breeding is the best bet for the breeder who wants to raise birds for the pet market. He wants average quality birds. He does not care about their ancestry and he wants to raise as many as possible.

After such a breeder has constructed one or more large aviaries or flight cages he gets good, healthy, quality stock birds, not show birds or birds of superior quality. These would be too expensive for his purposes and for his market. He turns a number of pairs of these birds into each aviary and lets them get acquainted and accustomed to their new surroundings for a few days. Then he puts nest boxes, two for every pair of birds, into the aviary. The extra boxes are to allow the hens a certain amount of freedom of choice as to nesting sites and thereby keep fighting among the hens at a minimum. All of the nest boxes are put as high as possible in the aviary and all are put at the same level.

An ideal commercial Parakeet hatchery. Photo
courtesy Orville Tutwiler

Within a few days the birds have begun to lay and it is just a question of time before there will be young birds in the nest boxes. If allowed to do so, the birds will raise nest after nest and some of the young will start raising their own families within just 5 or 6 months. You would hate to have a bird, even as a pet, that had come from such an aviary, however. The reputable breeder will not allow his birds to raise more than two or three nests per year and will take out the young birds when they are able to fend for themselves so that they cannot start raising their own families while still too young. The breeder who is too eager to get large quantities of young will soon find that he sacrifices the health of his birds when he works them too hard at raising family after family. It is just a question of time before his aviary will be stricken with disease and he will soon be out of business. Such breeding practices are not only dangerous to the health of the birds but some of the diseases to which Budgerigars are subject are also communicable to man so that a poorly run aviary can be a real hazard to the health of the community in which it is located. There is no danger whatever from a well-run aviary.

In aviary breeding careful attention and good breeding practices will pay rich dividends in healthy birds and good quality young. It is next to impossible to consistently breed first quality show stock by the aviary method because controlled heredity is inevitably uncertain. Still by careful attention and sound sanitary habits good quality birds for the pet trade can be produced.

CAGE BREEDING

The hobbyist or fancier who wants to produce top quality birds for the show bench or who is interested in color breeding will have to know with absolute certainty the parentage of his young birds. The only practical way to do so is to keep each breeding pair in a separate cage alone. This method of breeding Budgies is commonly known as *cage breeding*.

The different types of cages that are used by different fanciers for cage breeding are almost as numerous as are the different types of cages in general use. Budgerigars are not hard to please when it comes to the quarters in which they live while raising their families. Although they need plenty of exercise during other times they seem to get by very nicely without exercise during the time when they are in the breeding cages. Be that as it may, their good nature should not be abused by putting them in quarters that are too small for them.

If you are building your own aviary and equipment you may wish to construct built-in breeding cages. In such a case build your breeding cages in rows and tiers with removable partitions so that when the partitions are taken out a larger cage to be used for a flight is at your disposal. However, many fanciers prefer to construct individual cages so that they can be moved about conveniently. The nest boxes can be placed either inside the cage or on the outside with the entrance hole opening into the cage. The cages should be constructed with metal or wooden frames and covered with hardware cloth of either ¼ or ½-inch mesh. Each cage should have a removable metal tray in the bottom so that it can be easily cleaned. This tray should be covered with paper (newspaper will do) and a generous amount of gravel should be spread on the paper. This gravel has a twofold purpose. First of all, Budgerigars,

A semi-commercial display in the basement of a private home.

like other birds, need gravel to help grind up their food. Secondly, the gravel on the cage floor helps to absorb the moisture in the droppings and thereby makes for a cleaner cage. A minimum size for a breeding cage, if you are constructing your own, is 2 feet long by 1 foot wide and 1 foot high.

If you do not wish to make your own cages there are a number of suitable manufactured cages on the market. Many of these are made specifically as Parakeet breeding cages. They are readily obtainable through your local pet shop. A more or less standard size in these manufatured cages seems to be 16 inches long by 10 inches wide and 9 inches high. These manufactured cages come equipped with two doors. One door is to facilitate the cleaning and the changing of food, water, etc. The other is at one end at the top. This is where the entrance to the nest box is attached. Most of these cages have removable seed and water cups and have a sliding tray on the bottom for the purpose of cleaning. These cages are obtainable constructed either of metal or of plastic. The metal is more durable and satisfactory. Plastic cages break, scratch and warp.

The seed and water cups that come with these cages are just about adequate if cleaned and refilled daily. Use both of them for water. For the seed use a flat dish placed on the floor of the cage. The seed husks are blown out of this and it is refilled with seed daily.

NEST BOXES

Nest boxes used for Budgerigars come in a variety of sizes and shapes. In the wild, Budgies nest in hollowed-out tree trunks or limbs. In captivity they have been induced to lay their eggs in any number of containers. Among the early favorites were coconut husks and gourds but it was found that the husks were ideal breeding places for mites while the gourds were difficult to clean. There are several kinds of nest boxes commonly in use today. Most of them are constructed of wood or plywood although some are made of cardboard and aluminum. Both the cardboard and the aluminum boxes have wooden blocks with concave depressions in the bottom.

It is impossible to say which design of nest box is the best. Actually most of them are quite similar in construction. The one most commonly used is constructed of plywood and is 6 inches square and 9 inches deep. The top lifts off. There is a removable block of wood about 1½ inches thick in the bottom of the box. It has a concave depression cut in it to keep the eggs from rolling about in the nest and getting broken. The entrance hole is about an inch from the top in the front of the box. It is about 1½ inches in diameter. There is a perch just below the entrance hole.

Budgerigars do not build nests. They lay eggs right on the bare wood.

The commercial type nest box (one side removed) available at most pet suppliers.

You may put about a tablespoon of sawdust on the floor of the nest box to help keep the eggs from rolling around but as often as not the hen will throw the sawdust out before she lays her first egg.

If you use the standard manufactured breeding cages you can fasten the nest boxes to them by means of the little screw hooks, obtainable at any ten cent or hardware store. Screw the hooks into the front of the nest box and then hang them onto the cage so that the entrance hole is right at the open door that is provided for that purpose.

The cages, nest boxes, feed dishes, etc., that your birds use should be kept clean as possible. The cages should have paper spread on the floor of the removable tray. Gravel should be put on this paper. The cages should be cleaned and the paper and gravel replaced at least three times a week except during the time when the hens are laying. It will not hurt anything for a cage to go uncleaned for a week or so during this time, two or three times a year.

The nest boxes should not need to be cleaned out while the birds are nesting unless the parents are particularly messy and red mites are found in the nest. In this case a thorough cleaning is in order.

Cages and nest boxes that have been used before should be thoroughly cleaned and disinfected at the beginning of the season before using them again. One good way of doing this is to saturate them thoroughly with boiling water into which has been put a liberal amount of good household disinfectant. After the cages and nest boxes are thoroughly dry dust some mite powder (obtainable at your pet shop) into all of the cracks and crevices and under the removable trays in the cages and under the concave blocks in the nest boxes. This will by no means guarantee that you will not have trouble with red mites but it will help to keep them at a minimum. It is a good idea to dust the mite powder under the feathers on the birds when setting them up for breeding.

Seed and water containers should be thoroughly washed at least once a week. The water containers should be rinsed out and refilled every day. Budgerigars are fond of putting seed husks, bits of green, paper, or anything else that is available into their water. This being true the water is quickly fouled and the dish needs rinsing and refilling at least every day.

Your cages and other equipment may need painting from time to time. Do not hesitate to paint but be sure to use enamel or some paint that does not contain lead or any other harmful chemicals. All birds are quite sensitive to lead and if a Budgerigar should pick off a little piece of paint containing lead and swallow it, he will surely be quite sick and he may die. Don't take that chance. It's not worth it.

The feeding of Budgerigars presents no problem for their diet is simplicity itself. In nature they are seed eaters. In addition they eat a few green foods such as grass and weeds of various types.

In captivity their diet should be basically the same thing—seeds and greens. It has been found that canary seed and millet make up the best readily obtainable diet for Budgies in captivity. White millet is higher in food value than the yellow or the red. As a matter of fact the red millet is practically worthless as far as food value is concerned. The usual mixture of canary and millet is half and half but this may be varied slightly one way or the other. Oats should be fed in a separate dish as a supplement to this diet. The amount of oats fed should be increased in cold weather and when the parents are feeding young birds in the nest.

There are a number of good commercial parakeet seed mixtures on the market. The average fancier will want to buy one of these mixtures instead of buying the seeds separately and mixing them himself. Some of these mixtures contain oats in which case it is unnecessary to feed oats in a separate dish as recommended above unless you desire to increase the ration of oats as you will during breeding season and in cold weather.

The pet owner or fancier who has only a few birds can get good parakeet seed mixtures in small quantities in almost any pet shop. The fancier who has a number of birds will find it considerably cheaper to order his seed in large quantities of 50 or 100 pound bags from his pet dealer.

In addition to the regular seed mixtures there are on the market a number of treat foods and dietary supplements of one kind or another. The treats provide a welcome variety from the routine diet and may be fed along with the canary and millet from time to time. They should be put in a separate dish. Many of the supplements contain valuable ingredients that will help to round out, balance, and supplement the regular diet. They are particularly valuable during the time the birds are breeding, raising young ones, and moulting.

In cold weather, before the birds are paired off for breeding, and while breeding and raising young, Budgerigars should be given cod liver oil. The cod liver oil should be mixed thoroughly with the seed, about one teaspoonful to a pint of seed. A few drops of wheat germ oil should also be mixed with each pint of seed.

The cod liver oil and wheat germ oil will not only help to build up both the breeding stock and the young and give them stamina but will also help to prevent egg binding in the hens.

Many fanciers soak some of their seed in water before feeding it to their birds. This is particularly advisable when your birds are feeding young as it is much more digestible and higher in food value than unsoaked seeds.

There are any number of good green foods that may be given to Budgies. Most any of the green leafy vegetables are good. You can use lettuce, celery and celery tops, beet tops and greens of carrot tops. In addition many weeds and grasses such as chickweed and dandelion may be given. The greens should be washed thoroughly before being given to your birds. Don't fail to do this. Some of the poisonous chemicals that are used in spraying vegetables will cling to the leaves and when eaten can cause serious illness or death to your birds. The greens should be put into the cage wet and with drops of water clinging to them. In the wilds Budgerigars bathe by rolling in the wet grass. They will do the same thing in a cage or aviary by rolling in the wet greens that you provide and then sitting on a perch and preening their feathers.

The greens that are left uneaten after a few hours should be taken out of the cage. If left they will spoil and not only foul up the cage but will make the birds sick if they eat them in their eagerness for green food. Greens should be fed at least every other day. If the birds are feeding young in the nest they should be fed every day.

The need for gravel has been pointed out in another connection. Gravel is an absolute necessity for Budgerigars. When ingested it becomes a vital part of the digestive system. It grinds up the food and in so doing performs the same function as teeth in higher animals. Birds can do without gravel for short periods of time but if deprived of it for very long they will soon sicken and die.

One other thing is necessary to insure your birds' health and that is a source of calcium such as cuttlefish bone, crushed oyster shell, or plaster board. It is from these souces that birds get the necessary minerals for the manufacture of bones, feathers, beak, toenails, and egg shell. One of these sources, cuttlebone, should be available at all times, particularly during the time when hens are laying and raising young.

At present several manufacturers are putting out a mineral block or brick which contains calcium and other minerals as well. These may be substituted for one of the above mentioned sources of calcium and, if anything, are better as many of them contain other beneficial ingredients.

One word of caution is in order here. *Budgerigars are seed eaters and vegetarians.* The diet given above is simple but adequate for them. You will never go wrong by adhering to it. The addition of other foods may bring trouble. The best diet is a simple one.

HOW TO TRAIN A BUDGIE

Much of what has been said elsewhere in this book has been devoted to the keeping and breeding of a number of Parakeets as aviary and cage birds. However, no book on Parakeets would be complete if it did not devote some space to the care, taming, and training of an individual Parakeet as a pet. Even the fancier who has a large number of breeders will want to tame an individual, teach it to say a few words, and teach it a few tricks. It is as pets that these little birds really come into their own. Indeed they have proved themselves to be such interesting and amusing companions that they have long since become America's most popular cage bird.

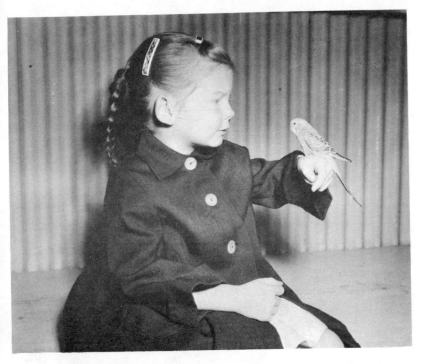

Budgies make wonderful pets for young and old alike.

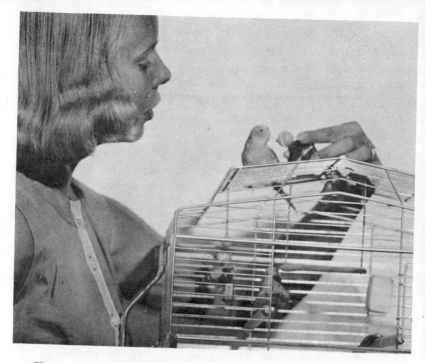

There are special toys available to assist you in training and entertaining your Parakeet. Photo by Mervin Roberts.

The best Budgie to get for a pet, either from your own aviary or from a pet dealer, is one that is just out of the nest box. If you intend to tame a Budgie to be a pet the younger you get him the better it will be and the more readily he will become accustomed to you and his new surroundings.

After you have chosen your bird a cage will be your next consideration. There are many good cages on the market and there is no point in trying to describe any of them here. They can be purchased at any pet shop.

If your bird is to spend all of his time in the cage it should be large enough for him to get a little exercise. On the other hand, if your bird will be given the liberty of the room for an hour or more every day then a smaller cage will suffice. Actually it is as a bird at liberty in the house that a pet Budgie is most amusing. He will ride about on his master's head or shoulder and will provide endless hours of mirth and amusement by his interesting antics. Many people leave the cage door open so that the pet bird can come and go as he pleases. The bird eats, drinks, and sleeps in the cage but spends most of the rest of the time sitting on a curtain rod, flitting about the room, or getting into some kind of mischief.

An ideal cage is placed on a stand and is fully equipped with the necessary watering, feeding and play accessories.
Photo by Mervin Roberts.

The cage may be put on a stand, hung on a bracket or placed on a table or some other piece of furniture. It should not, however, be placed on the floor, as Budgies seem to be happier if they are some distance above the floor. Care must be taken to place the cage somewhere out of a draft and out of the direct rays of the sun. Budgies are subject both to colds and to sunstroke, *either of which may be fatal.*

The ease with which you are able to train your bird and teach him to talk or to do tricks depends to a large extent on the tameness of the bird. Of course training and taming will depend to a great extent on the intelligence, disposition and capabilities of the individual bird. To an even greater extent it will depend on the patience and skill of the trainer.

The first step in training your Parakeet is taming it. You cannot train a wild bird. To tame your bird you must first win its confidence. The bird must know that you do not intend to harm it when you enter the room or approach the cage.

(A new bird should be allowed to rest and become accustomed to its surroundings for a day or two before any effort is made to tame it.)

One of the first steps in taming a bird is to put it in a place where it will have the frequent company of people. In this way it will become accustomed to human companionship.

After the first day make it a point to be around the cage as much as possible and to talk to the bird in quiet and reassuring tones. Do not make any quick movements around the bird but move slowly and deliberately. Place your hands on the cage from time to time, all the while talking to the bird. After the bird has become accustomed to this routine, open the cage door slowly and put your hand inside. Repeat this several times a day for the next few days. Soon your Budgie will become accustomed to your hand and will perch upon your extended finger.

One bit of useful knowledge that is frequently overlooked in the taming of any bird or animal is the power of hunger and the use of food in obtaining the confidence and overcoming the natural fear that the bird or animal has of humans. It is not meant that you should starve your bird unnecessarily, but when your Budgie learns that you are the one to whom it must look for food, it will come to have confidence in you more quickly. If a hungry bird has the choice of eating out of your hand or not at all it is likely to eat out of your hand. Do not overdo this to the point where you endanger your bird's health or make it too uncomfortable. In an extremely wild bird fear is a more powerful drive than hunger.

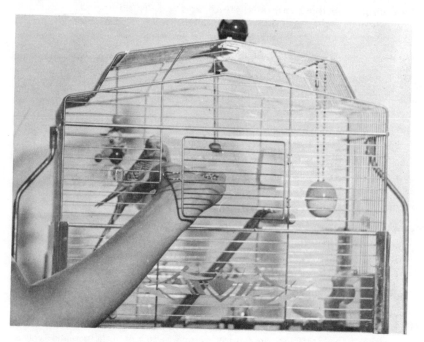

Attempt to train your pet Budgie to accept food from your hand.
Photo by Mervin Roberts.

A young Budgie is easier to train than an old one. Normally the stripes on the forehead denote an immature specimen (left) while a clear forehead signifies that the bird is mature.
Photo by Mervin Roberts.

One of the best ways to use the hunger drive to advantage is to take all food out of the cage after your bird has had his evening feeding. Budgerigars are in the habit of eating the first thing in the morning so with food unavailable to your bird until you replace it he will get pretty hungry. Do not wait too long to replace the food but when you do so let your hands linger around the feed dish for a few moments. Repeat the procedure for a few days and then, some day when you have a little extra time, put the feed dish within your Parakeet's reach and keep it in your hand. Eventually, depending on how hungry and how afraid he is, your Parakeet will eat out of the dish that you are holding. Do not make a sudden movement or a loud noise while doing this or you will undo all that you have done.

After your bird has become thoroughly accustomed to your hand, whether you use the hunger method of taming or just use gentleness and persuasion, put your hand in the cage and press your index finger gently but firmly against your Budgie's chest. This will throw him off balance so that he will either have to step onto your finger or fly to another perch. It is just a question of time until he will be stepping onto your finger and he will soon get on your finger any time you put it within his reach. When you have reached this point it is time to take your bird out of the cage into the room for the first time.

The first time you take your bird out of the cage should be at night so that you can turn out the light and catch him easily. The first time out he will probably fly rapidly and excitedly about the room. *DO NOT CHASE HIM!* To do so would undo all of your previous taming. Let him fly about and exhaust himself; then see if he will get on your finger. If he will not then turn out the lights and you will be able to catch him easily without frightening him unduly. After a few times out of the cage he will steady down and no longer fly about aimlessly, but will come to you. After a while he can be allowed to stay out most of the time if you have a closed room in which to keep him. Be careful about open doors and windows or he will escape and get lost.

Parakeets that have lost their fear of man also seem to lose fear of other things as well so you will have to be careful with such hazards as electrical fans, stoves, heaters and water.

Some people may advise you to clip the flight feathers on one wing so the Parakeet will be unable to fly until the feathers are replaced by new ones. Although this may be an aid in taming don't do it. A bird that cannot fly is at the mercy of a dog or cat and may even be stepped on because it cannot get out the way quickly enough. The power of flight is the only defense and escape that a Budgie has. To deprive it of this is to leave it helpless.

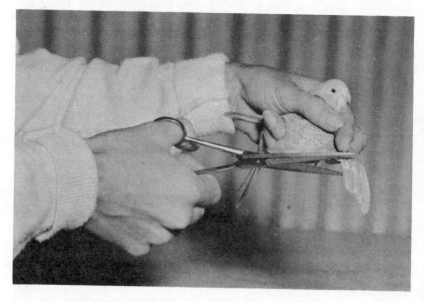

Have an expert cut the flight feathers on one wing if you are having difficulty in training your Parakeet.

A constant repetition of short phrases is the key to the successful training of a Budgie to talk. Photo by Mervin Roberts.

TEACHING YOUR BUDGIE TO TALK

The first thing every new Budgie owner asks is: "How do I teach my bird to talk?" The answer is simple: "Patience." You teach your bird to talk by repeating over and over to him what you want him to learn to mimic. You can start doing this while you are still in the process of taming your bird. In teaching a bird to talk, repeat the word or phrase (it is better to start with a single word) over and over as often as you can. Say it the first thing in the morning and after the lights are out at night. Repeat it every time you can and soon your bird will reward your patience by repeating it after you. Then is the time to start a new word. The more a bird learns the more quickly it learns. Actually you are teaching it to learn.

During the past few years a number of phonograph records have appeared on the market for the purpose of assisting in teaching your Parakeet to talk. These records can be used very effectively. They should be played over and over within the range of your bird's hearing. One advantage of using the record method of teaching is that the record can be played over and over by use of an automatic changer while you are away or are busy at something else.

A pet Budgie almost becomes a member of the family and should be taught names and phrases that have some significance to the family. This is not possible when you teach your bird to talk by means of a record unless, of course, you make a record yourself containing family names and significant phrases.

An important thing to remember is that birds kept alone can be tamed and taught to talk more readily than those kept in the presence of other birds. If you are trying to tame and teach more than one bird you will have more success if you keep them in separate cages. It would be better if they were not even kept in the same room. If there are other birds present the bird you are trying to tame will not become dependent on human companionship but will rely on the other bird or birds for companionship. After the birds are thoroughly tamed and trained it will not do any harm to keep them together.

The best way to teach your Budgie tricks is by rewarding a good performance with praise and a favorite food. Birds can be taught many of the same tricks dogs or other animals learn, such as to play dead or to shake hands. When they have been shown what is expected of them they should be rewarded for a good performance.

Many of the so called "tricks" that Budgies do are in reality a result of their natural mischievousness and curiosity. Their ability to play with toys is evidenced to by the numerous Parakeet toys that there are on the market at present.

When my little girl was a baby we had a pet Budgie that would fly down to the bathinette and bathe with her every morning. If his cage door was closed at bath time he would protest loudly until someone opened it for him.

Another Parakeet we had was fond of following my wife when she was sewing. He would come along behind her and remove each pin just after she put it in the material.

Anyone who has had a pet Budgie could tell a dozen similar stories. They are amusing little birds and make fascinating pets.

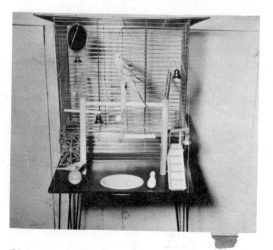

A nice cage equipped with a "gym" will assist you in training your Budgie to do tricks.

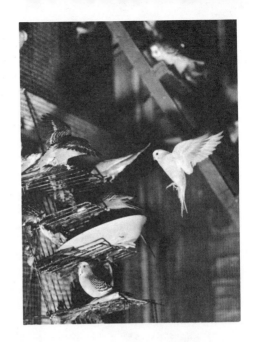

The fate of a Parakeet lies in the hands of its owner. It is up to the individual to provide the necessities of life for their bird.

HOW TO KEEP YOUR PARAKEET HEALTHY AND HAPPY

Budgerigars are not delicate but normally healthy, hardy creatures that get along with a minimum of care and attention. Like everything else they do require certain conditions and a certain diet if they are to remain healthy and happy. Most birds and animals are susceptible to some illnesses and accidents. It can be truthfully said, however, that most of the illnesses and accidents to which the majority of them fall victim are due to some cause that could be avoided by good aviary management.

The important aspects of the raising and keeping of Parakeets has been dealt with at one place or another in the earlier chapters of this book, but can be summarized briefly here in the five commandments of a Budgie owner:

1. Provide quarters that are dry, where your Budgie can get out of drafts and the direct rays of the sun. Avoid places that are subject to heat or cold.

2. Do not allow your Budgies to raise more than two or at the most three nests of young per season.

3. Allow the birds plenty of flight space and exercise when not breeding and raising young.

4. Keep their quarters clean.

5. Give a simple but well-balanced diet of seeds and greens.

There is much more that could be said regarding the maintenance of health and well-being of your birds but most of it is pretty well summed up in the five points above.

Budgerigars are reasonably long-lived. Their normal life span is somewhere between 6 and 10 years with 7 years being about the average.

Although the maladies from which Budgies may suffer are not numerous by any means, there are a few illnesses that you should know something about. Of primary importance in treating any sick bird, no matter what the cause of his illness: *a bird should be kept warm.* It cannot be emphasized too strongly. The body temperature of birds is higher than that of many other animals and when they are sick and run down a chilling can be disastrous. If possible raise the air temperature to 85° or 90° for a sick bird. This may be done by putting the bird into a box in which has been placed a large light bulb. The bulb will give off enough heat to keep the box warm. The bulb may be covered with wire and that in turn covered with a cloth of some kind to prevent the sick bird from burning himself and to keep the intense light from making him uncomfortable.

A sick bird afflicted with French Moult.

When colony breeding is your technique, you must be extremely careful to guard against contageous diseases.

Several of the pet supply companies have put out hospital cages that are equipped with heating units, thermometers and thermostats. These cages are, of course, ideal for keeping a sick bird and are reasonably inexpensive. Veterinarians and pet shop managers often specialize in curing sick birds. Consult them.

DISEASES OF PARAKEETS

Colds and Pneumonia — If your bird develops colds it is usually because he has been placed where he could not get out of a direct draft. An untreated cold can quickly turn into pneumonia. The first thing to do is to keep your bird warm. If he is wheezing, sneezing and coughing, the medicated vapor from a vaporizer or a tea kettle may make him more comfortable. Your local pet shop or veterinarian can supply you with a medicine containing penicillin or some other antibiotic that should help to clear up the cold or pneumonia. A small amount of this medicine may be placed in the bird's beak with a medicine dropper and some more of it should be added to the drinking water.

Diarrhoea — When suffering from diarrhoea a Budgie's droppings are loose and watery. Often the bird is listless and sits on a perch with his feathers ruffled. He may even keep his head under wing. In treating a diarrhoea-afflicted bird first of all keep him warm. All green food should be discontinued and a diarrhoea remedy obtained from your pet dealer or veterinarian. Most of the remedies obtainable now contain either one of the sulfa drugs or an antibiotic. Diarrhoea can be very dangerous and should be brought under control as quickly as possible.

Sometimes a normal moult is confused with French Moult. Compare the bird to the one perched on the breeding box on page 56.

French Moult — French moult is a feather disease afflicting young Budgerigars just after they leave the nest box. Some or all of the primary wing feathers and long tail feathers are malformed and fall out. The feathers that replace them are often diseased as well.

The exact cause of French moult is unknown. Some authorities say that it is caused by a particular kind of mite while others say that it is the result of a dietary deficiency. In all probability anything that would sap the strength of the young birds at a time when the feathers are being formed might have some influence on the formation of the feather structure. Without knowing the exact cause it is also difficult to know a cure. Some cases clear up of their own accord — others appear to be incurable.

Care should also be taken to feed a good diet. One of the dietary supplements may help.

Egg Binding — Occasionally a hen will get egg bound and be unable to pass an egg that she is attempting to lay. She will be quite obviously in severe pain and will probably squat on the cage floor unable to fly. Her lower abdomen is swollen and the position of the egg is obvious. Unless she eventually passes the egg she will surely die.

An egg bound hen should be kept warm. Sometimes giving her a drop of cod liver oil in her beak and painting the vent with cod liver oil will help her to pass the egg. Hold her so that steam from a kettle can warm her vent. This will relax the muscles sufficiently for her to pass the egg.

If she is unable to pass the egg for several hours and it is a question of doing something or losing a valuable bird you will have to take matters into your own hands and "deliver" the hen of her egg.

When you pick up an egg bound hen and turn her over you can see the outline of the egg in the lower part of her abdomen just in front of the vent. The egg itself will probably not be visible but you can feel it when you press gently on her abdomen with your fingers.

Before you pick up an egg bound hen to deliver her egg it is well to put on gloves so that she cannot bite your hand. Hold the hen firmly and place thumbs or forefingers just in front of the egg and press gently but firmly in the direction of the vent. Gradually increase the pressure in your fingers until the egg with the binding membranes clinging to it is slowly pushed from the vent. Most of the egg will still be covered by the membranes but at the end there will be a small opening where the egg itself will be visible. Starting at this opening gradually work the membranes back until about a third of the egg is exposed. At this point stop and paint the exposed membranes with mercurochrome or some other *mild* antiseptic to avoid infection. Then finish working the membrane

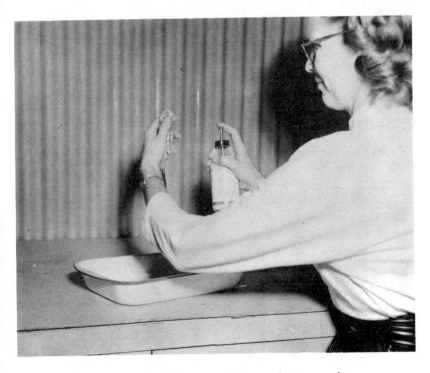

Spray your Budgie to protect against parasites.

back until the egg is freed. This is a last resort measure but it has been used successfully a number of times to save valuable hens.

After the hen is delivered of her egg, whether voluntarily or otherwise, she should be put in a cage alone and kept warm for several days. Then she can be returned to a flight cage. It is not advisable to try to breed her again until the next season.

Actually, though egg bindings is not uncommon it is, in most cases, unnecessary. It can be avoided by giving the bird seed treated with cod liver oil as described in the section on feeding.

Psittacosis or *Ornithosis* — This is a respiratory disease that was first discovered in parrots but occurs in other birds and barnyard fowls as well. It is communicable to man. Actually, although it has been the subject of a lot of sensational and uncalled for publicity, it is quite rare. It responds in birds and men alike to several of the new antibiotic drugs. If you fear this disease has affected you, consult your physician. Ornithosis in man is symptomatically an atypical pneumonia. It is rarely fatal.

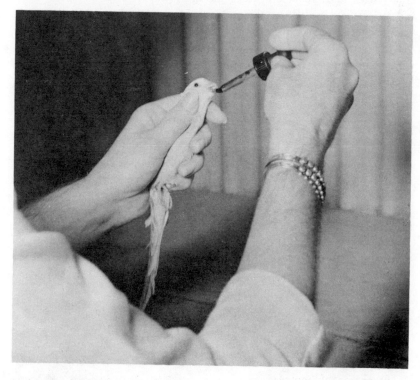

Hold the Parakeet's head between your thumb and index finger in this manner to administer a liquid medicine in a dropper.

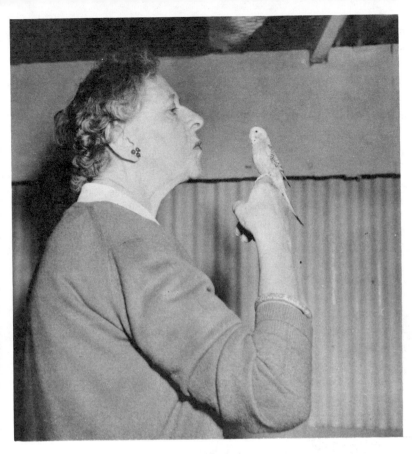

Success with Budgies is up to you!

AMERICAN BUDGERIGAR SOCIETY'S
41 POINTS TO SUCCESS

1. Always buy the best birds you can afford. It costs the same to feed a good bird as a bad one.

2. When building a new aviary, always have concrete floors; this 12" deep, with ¼" wire netting as a floor with a metal drawer pan will keep out mice and rats and facilitate cleaning.

3. Breed in cages. A nice size cage is one that is 36" long, 18" high, under the wire netting. This prevents young birds from picking up things not intended for them to eat. Pan slides in as a drawer and can be removed for cleaning. Cages can be built in sections, one to fit on top of another.

4. Water fountains should be above perches, not on the floor.

5. Perches that are not firmly fixed and are too smooth will lead to many clear eggs and will often cause one to discard a hen, thinking she is barren when the trouble lies in the perches. One perch at each end of the size cage described above is plenty. Too many perches interfere with wing exercise. One perch should be smaller than the other. A change rests the bird's feet.

6. Hang your nest boxes as high as possible and on the outside of the cage, at one end, not on the front. A perch and entrance hole can be cut in the end of the cage. Perch should extend 2" into the nest box.

7. When your pairs are on their last round and their youngsters are about two weeks old, remove the hen; the cock will rear the youngsters, and the hen will not lay another clutch of eggs.

8. Never take more than two rounds of youngsters from one pair of birds in one year, and never let any pair rear more than four young at one time; there is enough rubbish about without mass production.

9. If a cock or hen should die when youngsters are in the nest, do not add another mate, as this will certainly result in the murder of the chicks. Leave the bird alone and he or she will rear the young.

10. Use coarse pine or cedar sawdust in your nest boxes; it helps to keep the nest warm, clean and dry. Renew sawdust when it becomes fouled. Coarse sawdust will not harm the chicks. Do not use sand in nest boxes.

11. Watch your chicks in the nest boxes. If the parents are wet feeders or just careless feeders, they are apt to clog the beaks of the chicks, and if not cleaned daily will cause deformed beaks.

12. There is no difficulty in closed banding your chicks. Band when chick is ten days old — the three long toes through the band — with your fingers squeeze the ball of the foot gently. This will straighten the toes and enable you to slip this band over the large joint. If you have any trouble, write one of our old breeders, who will be pleased to help you. Always use A.B.S. closed bands. These will permanently identify you and your birds.

13. Always separate your sexes when not breeding; it is then easier to pair your birds when breeding season arrives.

14. Do not colony-breed. Infidelity in Budgerigars is a well-established fact.

15. Keep accurate records of the pedigree of every bird. This will pay big dividends in years ahead.

16. Budgies need lime. They get a small amount from hard water, but the amount is insufficient; give them a cuttlefish bone, a piece of

old plaster, or a nibble made of one part slaked lime and two parts of clean washed river sand. Let the nibbles set two months before giving to your birds.

17. Budgies also need grit, one part oyster shell, one part ocean or river sand to provide minerals. A sprinkling of ground charcoal is also an aid to digestion. Sterilized egg shells pulverized in a food chopper or old coffee grinder are also very good.

18. Green food is essential to your Budgies' health; see that it is fresh. Crushed or wilted greens have lost their vitamins. Carrots, beet-root, spinach, celery stocks and leaves, dandelion, plantain seed spikes, white clover and lawn clippings are all good. A piece of lawn sod cut 1½″ thick, turned upside-down in your flights so the Budgies can eat the earth and roots, is of great benefit. Earth kills germs and prevents disease rather than being harmful. When we say earth we do not mean filth.

19. Do not buy cheap seed; see that the seed has been recleaned. Buy only large plump seed. The cheapest seed is sometimes the most expensive, containing blighted grains and foreign seed. 40% plain canary seed and 60% yellow or white Proso millet is a good mixture. We do not recommend red millet. Feed one teaspoonful of cod liver oil stirred well into two pounds of seed while the birds are raising young and during the winter months while the birds are indoors. The best grade of hulled oats (oat groats), *white in color*, is a great help while the young are being fed and during the winter months. Oats should be discontinued during warm weather unless young are being reared. Feed oat groats in separate feed pots.

20. Budgies will breed any time, but they should not be permitted to start breeding until both the cock and hen are in the very best condition—free of all signs of moult. They should not be mated during the hot summer months and during the fall months when they should be putting on a new coat of winter feathers. To do so is to go against nature.

21. Don't expect your birds to win prizes in the shows if you do not train them, as a bird that is wild or afraid will spend most of its time on the floor of the cage or moving so fast it cannot be judged.

22. See that your show cages are nicely enameled and perfectly clean, and free from dust. Otherwise, your birds will have dirty heads.

23. Budgies cannot be properly trained in large cages. Get them acquainted with the show cage as soon as possible. Use A.B.S. Standard Show cages.

24. It has often been said that the judge should judge the bird and not the cage, but please remember that the public and fellow fanciers judge you by the way you stage your birds.

25. When the show is over, take care of your cages. Wash them thoroughly. If your shipping trunks are not dust-proof, wrap the cages in old newspapers and store. Remember show cages are expensive.

26. Spray your birds with cold water. It is a good tonic, it tightens the feathers and helps keep them fit. If you can use rainwater so much the better, as it puts a beautiful sheen on the feathers.

27. After spraying your birds, don't sweep the bird room as this will not improve the condition of the bird's feathers.

28. After spraying, transfer the birds to clean, dust-free cages to dry.

29. Make sure that windows and doors of your aviary are covered with wire netting. It prevents birds escaping should they get out of cages.

30. Flight cages are a necessity. Young birds and old birds when not breeding should be provided with large flights. The Budgie is a bird of swift flight and should have ample room to exercise. It develops proper wing carriage, size and disease-resisting birds.

31. During the summer when the birds are not mating, move them to outdoor flights if possible. Sunshine builds strong healthy birds. A shelter at one end of the flight should be provided to protect the birds from the hot sun.

32. Arrange your outdoor flight so the Budgies can get out into the rain. They enjoy it and it is good for them.

33. Don't grumble if you are beaten at the show, as there is no disgrace in it. Better to be a good sport.

34. The shows help us to correctly appraise our birds and to gauge our yearly progress with them.

35. If you have just cause for complaint in the show, inform the officials concerned and follow the rules set out in the Club Show Catalog. Don't lose your temper; discuss the matter in a gentlemanly or lady-like manner.

36. Don't blame your competitors. They are not responsible. They like to win as well as you.

37. Talk about birds, not other members of the Fancy.

38. Don't discredit the officers of the Society. They do what they do for nothing and in their spare time. Don't forget you may not know all the facts.

39. Be a worker and not a drone.

40. Be helpful to the beginner.

41. Smile.